Geek Out!

THE MODERN NERD'S GUIDE TO DRONE RACING

BY RYAN NAGELHOUT

Gareth Stevens
PUBLISHING

Please visit our website, www.garethstevens.com. For a free color catalog of all our high-quality books, call toll free 1-800-542-2595 or fax 1-877-542-2596.

Cataloging-in-Publication Data

Names: Nagelhout, Ryan.
Title: The modern nerd's guide to drone racing / Ryan Nagelhout.
Description: New York : Gareth Stevens Publishing, 2018. | Series: Geek out! | Includes index.
Identifiers: ISBN 9781538212011 (pbk.) | ISBN 9781538212035 (library bound) | ISBN 9781538212028 (6 pack)
Subjects: LCSH: Airplane racing–Juvenile literature. | Drone aircraft–Juvenile literature.
Classification: LCC GV759.N34 2018 | DDC 797.5'2–dc23

First Edition

Published in 2018 by
Gareth Stevens Publishing
111 East 14th Street, Suite 349
New York, NY 10003

Designer: Sarah Liddell
Editor: Joan Stoltman

Photo credits: Cover, p. 1 (left drone) marekuliasz/Shutterstock.com; cover, p. 1 (right drone) MikeDotta/Shutterstock.com; texture used throughout StrelaStudio/Shutterstock.com; p. 5 Jacob Lund/Shutterstock.com; p. 6 Juli112/Shutterstock.com; p. 7 Stahlkocher/Wikimedia Commons; p. 9 springart/Shutterstock.com; p. 11 (top) studioworkstock/Shutterstock.com; p. 11 (bottom) SVIATLANA SHEINA/Shutterstock.com; pp. 13, 17, 20, 25 Drew Angerer/Staff/Getty Images News/Getty Images; p. 14 Sean Gallup/Staff/Getty Images News/Getty Images; p. 15 Bloomberg/Contributor/Bloomberg/Getty Images; p. 18 Evgenyananiev/Shutterstock.com; p. 19 Christian.dk/Shutterstock.com; p. 21 Golubovy/Shutterstock.com; p. 23 Dan Istitene/Staff/Getty Images Sport/Getty Images; p. 27 MacFormat Magazine/Contributor/Future/Getty Images; p. 29 Education Images/Contributor/Universal Images Group/Getty Images.

Printed in the United States of America

CPSIA compliance information: Batch #CW18GS: For further information contact Gareth Stevens, New York, New York at 1-800-542-2595.

CONTENTS

Words in the glossary appear in **bold** type the first time they are used in the text.

FLYING AROUND THE TRACK

Imagine racing around a track at speeds of 70 miles (113 km) per hour while flashing lights show you where to go. Are you picturing a cool video game or maybe a racing scene from Star Wars? What if this wasn't something on a computer or in the movies? What if it was real?

Is it some kind of superfast go-kart racing? No! It's an entirely new kind of sport called drone racing! Let's explore the world of drone racing, how it got started, and some of the **technology** used to play this amazing sport.

WHAT IS A DRONE?

A drone is any kind of moving machine that doesn't have a pilot on board. Another word for this is "driverless." Some drones can fly using spinning blades, called **propellers**. Others move around on wheels like cars or small carts. They can fit in your hand or be as big as an airplane!

This picture shows how drone operators control their drones remotely, or from another location.

PILOTLESS HISTORY

Creating the technology needed to move **vehicles** and airplanes remotely took many years. One of the first drones was made by Serbian inventor Nikola Tesla. In 1898, he showed off a small boat that seemed to change direction when he talked! In fact, Tesla used radio waves to control the boat during an exhibition at Madison Square Garden in New York City. Most early drones were only used by the military for war. Racing them for sport is actually pretty new!

Today, drone technology is changing quickly. Drones are getting smaller, lighter, and smarter! This means there are more ways to use drones than ever before!

Today, drones can be used on farms, in war, and even by photographers to take pictures from high above!

THE RADIOPLANE

The first true drones were small model airplanes used for target practice. A former British pilot named Reginald Denny made nearly 15,000 "Radioplanes" for the US Army during World War II. The army practiced shooting at airplanes using these "Radioplanes" as targets!

TAKING FLIGHT

There are different kinds of drones, but the ones used in racing are called quadcopters. "Quad-" means 4, so these drones are named for the fact that they have four propellers, each with their own motor. When the propellers spin, they move the air around in a way that lets the drone lift off the ground.

Quadcopters are operated using a remote control that manages the speed the blades spin and how they move. Learning how to use the controls of the drone is the first thing a drone racer needs to do.

ROLL, PITCH, YAW, AND THROTTLE

There are different names for the way a drone moves. Roll means the movement left or right. Pitch tilts the drone, which moves it backward or forward. Yaw is the movement of a drone that spins it clockwise or counterclockwise. Throttle is the power that makes the propellers spin.

A QUADCOPTER REMOTE CONTROL

It's important to practice with your remote control as much as possible. You need to get your hands used to the movements needed to win a drone race!

ANTENNA

RIGHT STICK
TROLS ROLL AND PITCH

LEFT STICK
CONTROLS YAW AND THROTTLE

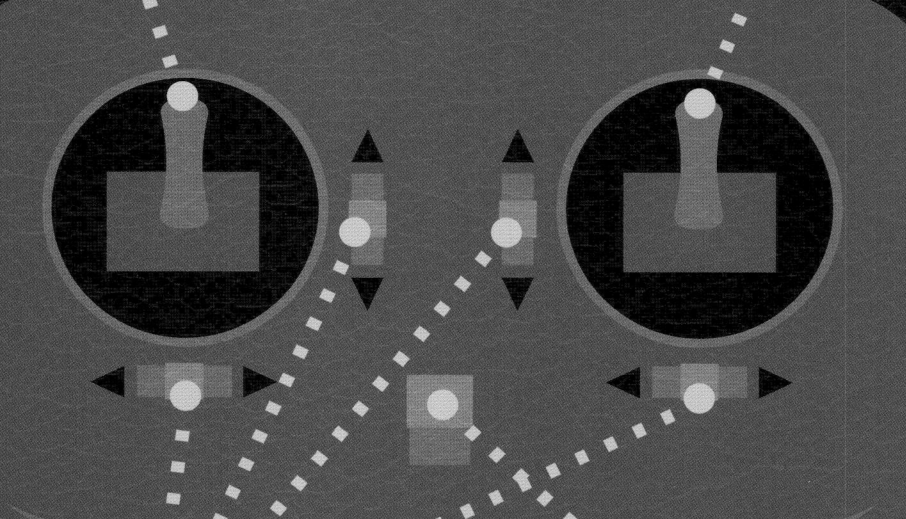

TRIM BUTTONS
BALANCE OTHER CONTROLS

POWER SWITCH

HOW IT ALL WORKS

Drones have batteries inside. This battery connects to the four motors, which each power a propeller. Commands are sent to the drone from the remote control, or transmitter, using radio waves. An **antenna** on the drone is the receiver, which takes in the communications from the transmitter.

The commands sent from the remote control are like directions to the drone. They're understood and managed by a part in the drone called the flight control board. This part then tells all the other parts of the drone what to do and when and how to do them.

HOW PROPELLERS LIFT

The shape of propeller blades on a drone helps it move air in a special way. The blades are twisted upward, instead of flat. When propeller blades spin, the twist in the blades makes the air pressure under the blade different from the pressure above the blade. This is called lift.

RACING DRONE

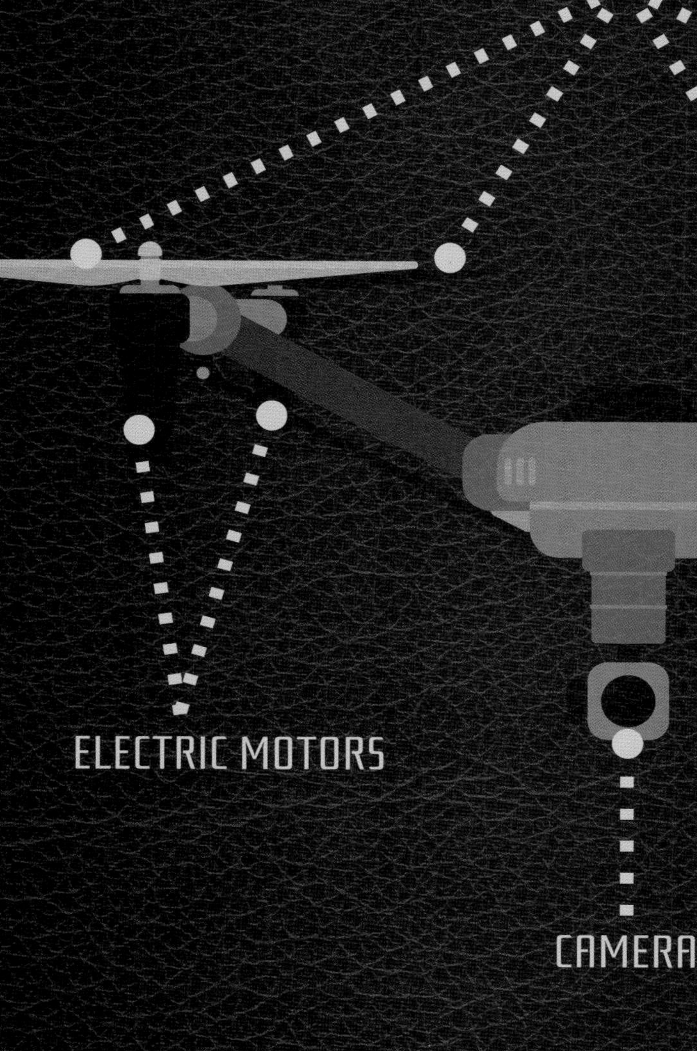

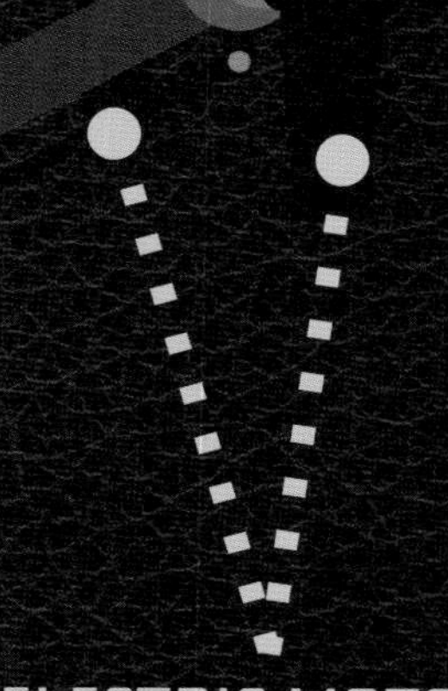

TOP VIEW

Flying drones are also called unmanned aerial vehicles (UAVs).

EYES IN THE SKY

Many drones are line of sight, which means their pilot sees them the entire time they fly. But racing drones fly in places their pilots can't see! They do this by using special cameras attached to the drone. The drone sends live video back to the pilot. The pilot wears special goggles to see just what the drone can "see." This is called first-person view, or FPV.

FPV drones quickly send video back to the pilot so they can **maneuver** around things. If a drone runs into something and the propellers stop spinning, the drone will fall out of the sky! Game over.

NOT IN HD

Drone goggles get video from the drone quickly, but it isn't always very clear. This is because lower-quality video can be sent from drone to goggles faster than clearer video. If there's a delay, or lag, in the video, the pilot can get **motion sickness**!

Without the technology to send video to the pilot, drone racing would be a very different sport!

SIZE AND SHAPE

Quadcopters are built on two different kinds of frames. One looks like the letter X, while the other is shaped like a plus sign. Racing drones, though, often look like the letter H. Racing frames can be made of a lightweight metal or a **material** called carbon fiber.

Racing leagues use drones that are similar in size to keep their **competitions** fair. Most racing drones fit into three size groups: Micro/150, Mini/250, and Open. The numbers are the distance between the drone's motors measured in millimeters. The smaller microdrones are often bought by beginners just getting into racing. They're best used indoors.

Bigger drones are heavier, so they need to have more powerful batteries to keep them in the air. Minidrone racing is the most popular form of drone racing.

MINIDRONES

OPEN RACING

Open racing has fewer limits on the size and **modifications** of its racing drones. Open racing drones can be up to 300 mm (11.8 in) and their propellers can be up to 6 inches (15.2 cm) long. This means the drones can be faster!

FLAGS AND HOOPS

There are several different kinds of races in the sport of drone racing. Races are set up on a course that's designed to test the pilot's skills and the drone's abilities in different ways. There are fast turns, **obstacles** to avoid, and even other drones that might get in the way!

Some races are time trials, which means drone pilots take a lap alone on a course to see who can go the fastest. Other races have multiple drones flying at the same time. Drones can be tested by flying through hoops or gates or by flying around flags.

DRAG RACING

Drag racing is a type of race where two drones fly against each other on a short course. The drones start motionless, then race to see who can cross the finish line first. Drag races aren't won just by speed but also by acceleration, or how fast a drone can get up to speed.

This drone racing competition held in New York City made pilots get their drones through hoops. Although it doesn't look easy, it sure looks fun!

MAKING CHANGES

Drones designed to take pictures usually have special parts that keep the drone balanced. They're also built to hover and have cameras on the bottom so they can get pictures while flying over things. But not racing drones!

Racing drones are built to only move forward. Their video camera is mounted on the front. All the special parts that help take a good picture are turned off so that pilots have more control over how the drone flies. Good pilots can make their racing drones make sharp turns and perform other **stunts** such as flips and spins. It takes a lot of practice, though!

Racing drones have special parts that manage the power that goes to a drone's engines. This lets them speed up or slow down quickly while in the air.

RACING DRONE

CAMERA DRONE

OUT OF THE BOX

An RTF, or ready-to-fly, drone means it can be bought and used right away. An almost-ready-to-fly, or ARF, drone, needs to be put together before it can be used. Most drones you can buy are either RTF or ARF, meaning you can get started racing without knowing how to build your own drone.

The best racing drones—the ones that the top drone racers use—are built, not bought. Once you've been flying a racing drone for a while and know what you want in a drone, you can modify, or change, it to make it better. Many drone pilots love trying new ways to get them to go faster.

Making a drone lighter makes it easier to lift off the ground so it can fly faster. Changing propellers can change how a drone lifts off. The position of the propellers on a drone can change how it flies. Experiment to see what works best!

It can take months to build a custom racing drone! However, you'll often end up with a better drone than one bought ready to fly.

GOOD GUTS

Everything in a racing drone can be modified to make it fly better. Batteries, motors, and electronic speed controllers can be switched out of an RTF or ARF to give drones more power. Even the type of goggles or the kind of controller used can change how you fly!

BE A CHAMPION

The top drone racers in the country compete in two different leagues. The Drone Sports Association hosts the US National Drone Racing Championships and the World Drone Racing Championships. In 2016, the Drone Racing League (DRL) started hosting big events. DRL events have even aired on ESPN and filled football stadiums!

DRL uses bigger drones and puts special lights on its racing drones so they're easier to see for fans. They also make pilots use drones with the same features, or specifications, to make sure they're competing in skill instead of drone features.

TAPE DELAY

DRL events are on TV, but they're not live. That's because they use special cameras to capture the action and put all the video together afterward before putting it on TV. Drone racing is exciting to watch, but it's often hard to follow the action while it's happening!

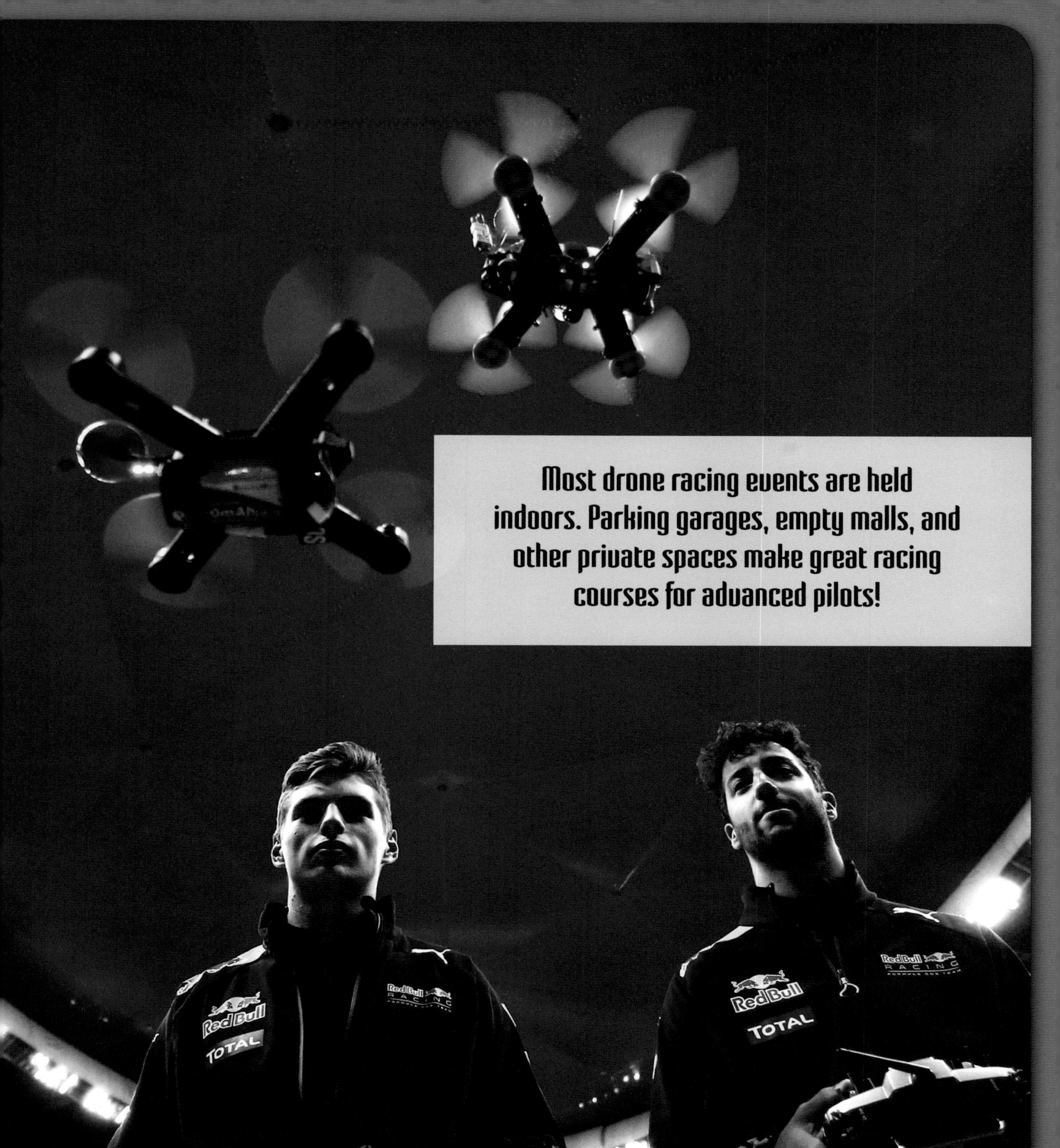

Most drone racing events are held indoors. Parking garages, empty malls, and other private spaces make great racing courses for advanced pilots!

DO IT YOURSELF!

Not all drone racing takes place in big stadiums with superexpensive, handmade drones. You can buy a small beginner drone and practice flying it for yourself! Plus, there are drone-racing clubs all over the country where people hold events to show off their skills.

Many people make their own courses to test their skills out at home, too. You can build gates using pool noodles. You can even set up obstacles to fly over and under to make the race more exciting. Host your own **tournament** with your friends!

FLY SAFE!

Always be careful when you're flying a drone. Make sure people or animals aren't nearby or below when you fly a drone. If it falls, it could hurt someone! You also have to make sure someone else isn't using the same radio channel you are!

More experienced fliers can win money at championship events. That helps them build better drones—building a winning racing drone can be expensive!

RACE ON LAND

Not all racing drones fly! Small remote control car drones also have FPV camera technology that allows drivers to race. Many of these smaller drones send video to a smartphone or tablet instead of to goggles. The phone's screen shows what the drone's camera sees—and can even be controlled by voice!

These small racing vehicles are even designed to jump! They have wide wheels to give them good grip on the ground and let them make quick turns like flying drones. These remote control car drones are fun to race with a friend. Make your own course using cardboard boxes, wood, and more!

ON WATER?

Most drone racing still takes place in the skies, but some companies are looking to race on water as well. A company called Parrot has a tiny drone that attaches to a boatlike vessel called a hydrofoil. When the drone is moving, the hydrofoil lifts out of the water!

Car drones can also do spins and flips. They're fun to race with others and are much cheaper than many flying racing drones.

THE FUTURE OF FLIGHT

As drone technology improves, the way we race drones will change. Improvements in camera technology will mean pilots can see better and avoid crashes, and their skills will improve. As more people take to the skies with drones, the competition to be the best will continue to heat up.

While some drone racers are going pro, it's important to remember that most people race to have fun! Most people just like to fly with their friends and enjoy testing their skills as a builder and a pilot. Do you think you have what it takes to join the race?

START SMALL

The first step in going pro is starting to race as a hobby. Try to find an event happening nearby to see how it's done. There are lots of drone-racing videos online that have great tips to help you get started!

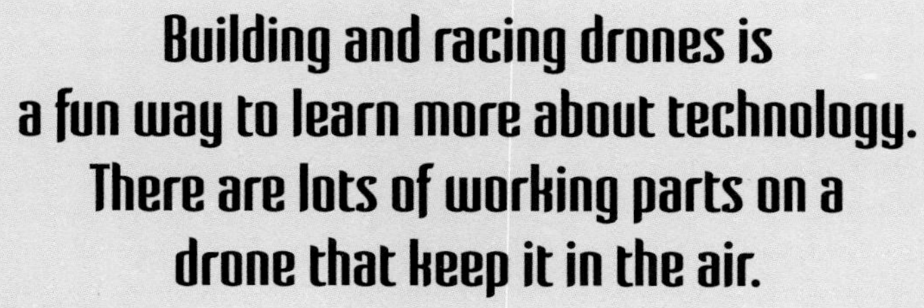

Building and racing drones is
a fun way to learn more about technology.
There are lots of working parts on a
drone that keep it in the air.

GLOSSARY

antenna: a usually metallic device for receiving radio waves

competition: an event in which people try to beat others

maneuver: moving safely to avoid hitting things

material: something used to make something, such as a fabric

modification: a change made in order to improve something

motion sickness: a sickness caused by motion

obstacle: something that blocks a path

propeller: a device with two or more blades that turn quickly and cause a ship or aircraft to move

stunt: a challenging feat done to gain attention

technology: the special tools used to do a task and the way people use those tools

tournament: a series of contests that involves many players or teams and that usually continues for at least several days

vehicle: an object that moves people or goods from one place to another, such as a car

FOR MORE INFORMATION

BOOKS

Faust, Daniel R. *Civilian Drones.* New York, NY: PowerKids Press, 2016.

Kallen, Stuart A. *What Is the Future of Drones?* San Diego, CA: Reference Point Press, 2017.

Marsico, Katie. *Drones.* New York, NY: Children's Press, 2016.

WEBSITES

Drone Racing League
thedroneracingleague.com
Find out more about drone racing on the official site of the Drone Racing League.

How to Fly a Drone
uavcoach.com/how-to-fly-a-quadcopter-guide/
Learn how to control a UAV with this guide.

Racing Drone Buyers Guide
bestdroneforthejob.com/drones-for-fun/racing-drone-buyers-guide-2/
Find the right racing drone for you with this great guide.

Publisher's note to educators and parents: Our editors have carefully reviewed these websites to ensure that they are suitable for students. Many websites change frequently, however, and we cannot guarantee that a site's future contents will continue to meet our high standards of quality and educational value. Be advised that students should be closely supervised whenever they access the Internet.

INDEX